HAZBIN HOTEL

BAR BOOK

HAZBIN HOTEL

BAR BOOK

DRINKS AND SNACKS FOR WAYWARD SINNERS

Foreword by Vivienne Medrano

Recipes by Thea Engst

Written by Jordan Alsaqa

INSIGHT EDITIONS

SAN RAFAEL • LOS ANGELES • LONDON

Contents

FOREWORD

Dear Sinners,

I'm no stranger to a good drink. I actually met Amir Talai, the voice of Alastor, in person for the first time mid-swig. I went to see him perform at his cabaret show in Los Angeles a few years ago, where there was a drink minimum. I defaulted to my drink of choice, a Long Island, and I definitely exceeded the minimum. By the time we met, I was quite happy and bubbly. He, teasingly, called me "sloppy," . . . which I, in turn, had Alastor call Adam in Season 1. There have been many drinks and fun stories since then—including my first hangover after the *Hazbin Hotel* pilot screening party back in 2019, an ill-fated bar night with Sam Miller where I threw up out of a rideshare, a moment forever immortalized in *Helluva Boss.* Drinks—be they boozy or not—are a way to celebrate and bring people together, which is, gratefully, something we've done quite a bit of in the past few years. Since creating *Hazbin Hotel* and signing it to stream on Amazon Prime, there have been so many unprecedented changes and milestones for me as both a showrunner and artist. From the one-night-only Broadway live show to the *Hazbin Hotel* x Animate Cafe pop-up in Tokyo, I've had a lot to celebrate—so much so that it sometimes doesn't feel real. My team's art, dedication, and skill have lived far beyond the screen. This book is a beautiful example of how much love and passion this show has inspired. It includes sixty-six recipes: cocktails, mocktails, and delicious bar bites inspired by the show's characters and settings. Whether you indulge in the sin of gluttony or prefer to practice the heavenly virtues, there's something for everyone—wayward souls and complicated winners alike. Who wouldn't want Beelzejuice IRL? Me personally, I'm trying The Hazbin's New Look. Sign me up for glitter and tequila! So cheers, Sinners! Just remember to always pace yourself and drink responsibly; after all, you don't want to end up bitching to the bartender all night.

Love,

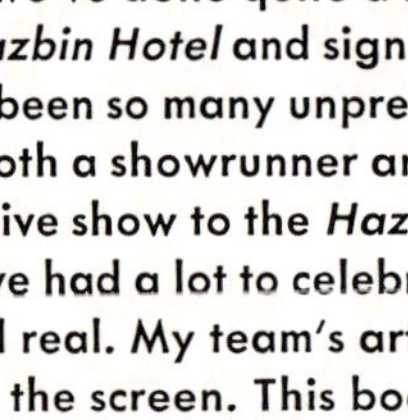

INTRODUCTION

Hell truly is other people in Pentagram City. From the various Overlords that happily rule over their fellow Sinners to the exorcists who come to annihilate the souls of the damned, every day in the underworld is an exercise in agony. Fortunately, even though they've been sentenced to eternal damnation, those Sinners can still forget their troubles with a stiff drink—it's Hell, after all. What better place to indulge in your vices?

From the sex-filled halls of Consent to the privacy of the Hazbin Hotel bar, you don't have to go far in Hell to find a drink, and the damned wouldn't have it any other way. With this cocktail book, we offer the finest selection of high-end cocktails and barroom booze from across the Pentagram, presented with far less violence, sex, and unidentified bodily fluids than you'd encounter on a trip to Hell itself. If you want any of that stuff, feel free to provide it yourself; we're not here to judge!

What we are here to do is provide all manner of delicious drinks to make the misery of existence go down a bit smoother. From virgin mocktails to high-spirited cocktails, we've got something for everyone—including a mix of drinks that go both ways, letting you enjoy a drink with or without the alcohol of your choice. Enjoy A Happy Day in Hell (page 64) that would make Charlie sing, take a shot of Something Strong (page 99) that'd help Angel Dust relax after a long day at the studio, or try to handle the power of Hell's elite by throwing back a The Bloody Overlords (page 56).

And don't worry, you won't need to put all that hooch on an empty stomach; we've also got a selection of snacks and apps to go with every drink. Feel free to stuff your face with as much food as you want; gluttony's a sin, but that sort of behavior's smiled upon in Hell! Indulge in some dipping and crunching with Niffty's Favorite Snack (page 120) or indulge like a winner with a plate of Adam's Ribs (page 129). Just be sure not to let Sir Pentious catch you chowing down on those Deviled Egg Boiz (page 123). And yes, many of these eclectic edibles were sourced from Cannibal Town, but we promise we've made the necessary replacements. What can we say, those flesh-eaters know how to season their meat!

So welcome to the *Hazbin Hotel Bar Book*! With a little bit of effort and our help, you'll have a song in your heart, a drink in your hand, and memories of Hell better than anyone who actually has to live there. Get your tumbler and swizzle sticks ready, turn the page, and remember: When you're here, you're a boozer, baby!

The Hotel's Bar Cart

TOOLS OF THE TRADE

BOSTON SHAKER

This is a two-piece cocktail shaker consisting of a large tin and a smaller tin, which, when fitted together, create a perfect seal so that you can shake your cocktail without leakage.

HAWTHORNE STRAINER

This is a standard cocktail strainer, made with a metal disk and a removable spring. Best for shaken drinks, it fits over a cocktail shaker to strain your drinks. Make sure yours has a removable spring so that you can make the homemade whipped cream recipes in here!

JULEP STRAINER

Best for straining stirred drinks, this strainer looks like a large spoon that's dotted with large holes and a small handle.

MIXING GLASS

The most classic version of a mixing glass resembles a large pint glass that's weighted and tapered at the bottom. You can have fun with choosing the look you like, though, as there are many elaborate, crystal options, too.

JIGGER

This hour-glass-shaped tool helps measure just how much alcohol you are pouring. It is two-sided; the larger side usually measures 1½–2 ounces (45–60ml) and the smaller side measures ½–1 ounce (15–30ml), although you can buy jiggers of different sizes.

BARSPOON

This spoon has a long handle, around 12 inches (30cm), and is used for mixing and layering drinks.

SYRUPS

SIMPLE SYRUP

½ cup granulated sugar

½ cup boiling filtered water (212°F)

Combine the sugar and water in a measuring cup or small mixing bowl and stir until cohesive. Once the mixture is cool, store it in a sealed container in the refrigerator for up to 1 week.

HONEY SYRUP

½ cup honey

½ cup boiling filtered water (212°F)

Combine the honey and water in a measuring cup or small mixing bowl and mix until cohesive. Once the mixture is cool, store it in a sealed container for up to 1 week.

CINNAMON HONEY SYRUP

½ cup honey

½ cup boiling filtered water (212°F)

2 cinnamon sticks

Combine the honey and water in a measuring cup or small mixing bowl and stir until cohesive. Break the cinnamon sticks into at least two pieces and stir them into the honey syrup. Allow to steep for at least 10 minutes or until cool; then strain. Once cool, store the mixture in a sealed container in the refrigerator for up to 1 week.

VANILLA ALMOND SYRUP

¼ cup boiling filtered water (212°F)

¼ cup granulated sugar

½ stick Madagascar vanilla bean, sliced open

1 barspoon almond extract

Combine the water, sugar, vanilla bean, and almond extract in a small mixing bowl. Stir until the sugar has dissolved; then let steep for 10 minutes. Strain the mixture through a fine-mesh strainer. Once cool, store the mixture in a sealed container in the refrigerator for up to 1 week.

AGAVE SYRUP

½ ounce agave syrup

½ ounce boiling filtered water (212°F)

Combine the agave syrup and water in a measuring cup or small mixing bowl and stir until cohesive. Once cool, store the mixture in a sealed container in the refrigerator for up to 1 week.

GINGER SYRUP

½ cup boiling filtered water (212°F)

½ cup granulated sugar

1-inch piece fresh ginger, peeled and chopped

Combine the water, sugar, and ginger in a small mixing bowl and stir until the sugar dissolves. Let the mixture sit for 20 to 30 minutes, or until cool. Strain and once cool, store the mixture in a sealed container in the refrigerator for up to 1 week.

BROWN SUGAR SYRUP

½ cup light brown sugar, unpacked

½ cup boiling filtered water (212°F)

Combine the brown sugar and water in a measuring cup or small mixing bowl and stir until cohesive. Once cool, store the mixture in a sealed container in the refrigerator for up to 1 week.

RASPBERRY SYRUP

1 cup fresh raspberries

1 cup granulated sugar

1 cup boiling filtered water (212°F)

In a medium-size bowl, gently break up the raspberries, add the sugar, and toss to coat. Let sit for 30 minutes; then add the water and stir. Strain and once cool, store the mixture in a sealed container in the refrigerator for up to 1 week.

BLACKBERRY SYRUP

½ cup fresh blackberries

½ cup granulated sugar

½ cup boiling filtered water (212°F)

In a medium-size bowl, gently break up the berries, add the sugar, and toss to coat. Let sit for 45 minutes; then add the water and stir. Strain and once cool, store the mixture in a sealed container in the refrigerator for up to 1 week.

NONALCOHOLIC (NA) SUBSTITUTES

NA "VODKA"

1 cup boiling filtered water (212°F)

2 bags Jasmine green tea

In a measuring cup, steep the tea bags in boiling water for 5 minutes. Remove them and let cool. Store the mixture in a sealed container in the refrigerator for up to 1 week.

NA PURPLE "VODKA"

1 cup boiling filtered water (212°F)

2 bags Jasmine green tea

1 tablespoon dried butterfly pea blossoms

In a measuring cup, steep the tea bags for 3 minutes; then add the butterfly pea blossoms in a loose-leaf tea strainer for 2 minutes more. Remove the tea bags and butterfly pea blossoms. Once cool, store the mixture in a sealed container in the refrigerator for up to 1 week.

NA "GIN"

½ cup boiling filtered water (212°F)

2 bags juniper tea

In a measuring cup, steep the tea bags for 5 minutes. Once cool, store the mixture in a sealed container in the refrigerator for up to 1 week.

NA "MEZCAL"

½ cup boiling filtered water (212°F)

1 tablespoon loose tea or 1 bag Lapsang souchong tea

In a measuring cup, steep the tea bags for 5 minutes before removing the bags or loose tea. Once cool, store the mixture in a sealed container in the refrigerator for up to 1 week.

ROOIBOS TEA-QUILA SUBSTITUTE

½ cup boiling filtered water (212°F)

2 bags rooibos tea

In a measuring cup, steep the tea bags for 5 minutes before removing the tea bags. Once cool, store the mixture in a sealed container in the refrigerator for up to 1 week.

BLACK TEA & FIG "BOURBON"

½ cup boiling filtered water (212°F)

1 bag black tea

¼ cup fig jam

In a medium-sized mixing bowl, steep the tea bag for 5 minutes; then add the fig jam. Whisk the mixture until the jam dissolves; then strain it through a fine-mesh strainer. Once cool, store the "bourbon" in a sealed container in the refrigerator for up to 1 week.

BLACK CURRANT "BOURBON"

1 cup boiling filtered water (212°F)

2 bags black tea

½ cup black currant jam

In a medium-sized mixing bowl, steep the tea bags for 5 minutes; then remove the bags. Add the jam to the tea and whisk until the jam is fully dissolved. Strain the mixture through a fine-mesh strainer. Once cool, store the "bourbon" in a sealed container in the refrigerator for up to 1 week.

INFUSED ALCOHOL

SEAWEED-INFUSED GIN

10 ounces London dry-style gin

1 sheet sushi nori, torn

In a jar, combine the gin and nori and shake. Let sit in a sealed container overnight at room temperature. Strain through a fine-mesh strainer. Store the mixture in a sealed container at room temperature indefinitely.

HIBISCUS VODKA

8 ounces vodka

2 tablespoons dried hibiscus

In a jar, combine the vodka and hibiscus and shake. Let sit in a sealed container overnight; then strain through a fine-mesh strainer. Store the mixture in a sealed container indefinitely.

SHRUB

APPLE SHRUB

1 or 2 small sweet apples, grated

1¼ cups granulated sugar

1 cup apple cider vinegar

½-inch piece fresh ginger, peeled and chopped

Combine the apples, sugar, apple cider vinegar, and ginger in a jar. Seal the jar and shake vigorously before placing it in the refrigerator for 4 days. On the fourth day, strain it through a fine-mesh strainer. Store the shrub in a sealed jar in the refrigerator for up to 1 month.

1

MOCKTAILS for Chumps!

LITTLE PRINCESS MORNINGSTAR

YIELD: 1 DRINK

When a prospective resident of the Hazbin Hotel walks through its doors, you can be sure that the first thing they'll see is the smiling face of its founder, Charlie Morningstar, welcoming them to the first day of the rest of their afterlives. Hell's princess wants to make sure every guest knows that, just because something is good for you, doesn't mean it can't also be a fun time. Similarly, this green drink packs plenty of nutritious vitamins within its sweet mixture of tropical flavors like passion fruit, ginger, and banana.

½ cup fresh spinach plus 3 leaves for garnish

½ cup passion fruit juice

¼ large or ½ small sweet apple

1-inch piece fresh ginger, peeled and chopped

⅓ cup plain Greek yogurt

1 banana, sliced, reserving 1 slice for garnish

1 slice starfruit

SPECIAL EQUIPMENT

Blender

In a blender, combine the spinach, passion fruit juice, apple, ginger, and yogurt. Blend until smooth; then pour the mixture into a tall glass.

Using a cocktail skewer, thread the starfruit slice, then the 3 spinach leaves, fanned out, and then the banana slice to hold the arrangement together. Garnish with the skewer and serve.

VAGGIE'S SECRET

YIELD: 1 DRINK

Charlie's biggest supporter in her mission to redeem Sinners is her girlfriend, Vaggie, who has spent a lot of her time struggling with a secret desire for redemption all of her own. Vaggie does her best to keep her angelic past hidden, but like the giant ice sphere in this mescal drink, secrets have a way of floating to the top. Still, love conquers all, and even through the hard times, Vaggie and Charlie know they can count on each other more than anything.

1½ ounces NA "Mezcal" (page 12)

1 ounce beet juice

¾ ounce Agave Syrup (page 11)

½ ounce lemon juice

One 4-ounce ice sphere

1 large, raw beet, peeled

SPECIAL EQUIPMENT

1 X-shaped cookie cutter

1 skewer

In a cocktail shaker filled with ice, add the NA "mezcal," beet juice, agave syrup, and lemon juice.

Shake well; then strain into a glass over the ice sphere.

Slice the beet into ½-inch-thick wheels. Using a small, X-shaped cookie cutter (about 1 inch wide), cut two shapes out of each wheel.

Skewer the beets, garnish, and serve.

OOH, HE'S A *GOOD* BOY!

YIELD: 1 DRINK

You can always count on the Hazbin Hotel's number-one support staff member Niffty to speak her mind. She's especially vocal about her appreciation for a bad boy, leaving her disappointed when Sir Pentious proves to be anything but. She'd probably have a similar reaction to this margarita; sure, it packs a punch with a mix of jalapeño and chile flavors, but as a mocktail, this one's for the good boys. Still, there's plenty of flavor to enjoy, and given what a lightweight Niffty is, probably best to keep hers alcohol-free regardless.

2 ounces Rooibos Tea-quila Substitute (page 12)

¾ ounce Agave Syrup (page 11)

½ ounce lime juice

½ ounce lemon juice

½ ounce pickled jalapeño brine

1 teaspoon Tajín, sprinkled on a plate

1 dehydrated red chile

1 lime wheel, scored

In a cocktail shaker filled with ice, add the rooibos tea-quila substitute, agave syrup, lime and lemon juices, and pickled jalapeño brine. Shake well.

Run the lime wheel halfway around the rim of a rocks glass, then dip the glass in the Tajín to coat half the rim.

Strain the drink over fresh ice cubes in the glass, garnish with the dehydrated chile and lime wheel perched on the rim, and serve.

Rosie's Sweet Tea

YIELD: 1 DRINK

For a place called Cannibal Town, this sector of Hell is surprisingly nice. That can be credited to the leader of the cannibals, Rosie, who does a remarkable job of keeping those flesh-eaters cordial and orderly. Rosie has a way of making all her subjects feel heard and respected, with a friendly ear and plenty of snacks to offer, courtesy of Rosie's Emporium. Though the food may be suspect at best, there's nothing like a warm cup of tea to soothe the soul after a long day, especially when it's filled with healing herbs like rosemary and basil. If it also helps pre-season a future meal, well, that's just a bonus for this Overlord.

½ teaspoon chopped fresh rosemary

½ teaspoon chopped fresh basil

2 lemon wheels

½-inch piece fresh ginger, peeled and sliced into wheels

¼ teaspoon honey

¾ cup boiling water (212°F)

1 rosemary sprig

SPECIAL EQUIPMENT

Loose-leaf tea strainer

1 match or lighter

Put the chopped rosemary and basil in a loose-leaf tea strainer and put it in a mug.

Express one lemon wheel and drop it in the mug. Add the ginger and honey.

Top with boiling water, let steep for 3 minutes, and then remove the tea strainer. Stir gently.

Push the rosemary sprig through the center of the remaining lemon wheel. Singe the sprig to create a smoky, herbal fragrance. Garnish and serve.

THE ZEEZI ZINGER

YIELD: 1 DRINK

Loud and passionate, with electric neon vibes and an intimidating stature, you can catch Zeezi in the club—her voice commands attention even over the pounding of the drum machine. With this frothy matcha mix, you can capture a bit of that bold personality in a drink that stands out from the crowd.

¼ cup matcha tea powder, plus 1 dash for garnish

¾ ounce pineapple juice

½ ounce Simple Syrup (page 10)

1 scant barspoon vanilla extract

2 ounces soda water

SPECIAL EQUIPMENT

Handheld milk frother or hand whisk

In a cocktail shaker or small mixing bowl, combine the matcha tea powder, pineapple juice, simple syrup, and vanilla. Mix well using a milk frother or a hand whisk.

Pour the mixture over ice into a large rocks or Collins glass and top with the soda water. Add a dash of matcha on top to garnish and serve.

EMILY'S PRECIOUS PUNCH

YIELD: 1 DRINK

Charlie's trip to Heaven isn't the most fruitful, but she does manage to find at least one sympathetic soul in Emily. This sweet-hearted seraphim sees the injustice being done to the damned, and though she doesn't have the strength to immediately turn on the will of her fellow angels, she gives Charlie hope. For Charlie's kindred spirit, this spirit-free cocktail captures a similar sweet flavor profile. And hopefully, Emily's tapioca pearls of wisdom can influence change in Heaven, or at least in your taste buds.

½ cup fresh blueberries

2 ounces NA "Vodka" (page 12)

½ ounce lemon juice

½ ounce Simple Syrup (page 10)

½ teaspoon purple tapioca pearls

4 ounces NA sparkling wine

In a cocktail shaker, muddle the blueberries. Add ice, the NA "vodka," lemon juice, and simple syrup.

Shake well; then double-strain into a champagne flute over the tapioca pearls.

Top with NA sparkling wine and serve.

Saint Peter's Solo

YIELD: 1 DRINK

When humans are deemed worthy of a blissful afterlife, they're greeted at the gates of Heaven by the million-dollar smile of Saint Peter. It's his job to show every guest, even the temporary ones like Charlie and Vaggie, just how great a place Heaven is. Emulating the sugary-sweet embrace of paradise, this mocktail captures the light, airy joy Peter hopes residents and visitors to Heaven will enjoy, cotton-candy clouds and all.

2 ounces purple NA "Vodka" (page 12)

1 ounce Simple Syrup (page 10)

½ ounce lemon juice

¼ cup blue cotton candy

In a cocktail shaker filled with ice, add the NA "vodka," simple syrup, and lemon juice. Shake well and strain into a coupe glass.

Garnish with cotton candy balancing atop the drink; drop it in immediately before enjoying the drink.

Katie Killjoy's Bad News

YIELD: 1 DRINK

The lead anchor for 666 News lives up to her name, delivering as much bad news as possible with a twisted smile and a sadistic glint in her eye. There's no telling what awful new info she's going to drop in her next report, so hopefully a nice cup of hot chocolate can ease the sting. This calming classic is given a strawberry spin to match the red hues of Katie's killer power suit. Oh, but be sure you let it cool down a bit before drinking it, because Katie sure won't care if you burn yourself.

STRAWBERRY HOT CHOCOLATE

1 teaspoon granulated sugar

½ teaspoon powdered sugar

1 teaspoon cocoa powder

¼ ounce strawberry syrup

¾ cup boiling water (212°F)

STRAWBERRY WHIPPED CREAM

2 ounces heavy (whipping) cream

½ ounce strawberry syrup

1 strawberry, scored

SPECIAL EQUIPMENT

Hawthorne strainer

TO MAKE THE STRAWBERRY HOT CHOCOLATE: In a mug, combine the sugars and cocoa powder (or use your favorite premade hot chocolate). Add ¼ ounce of strawberry syrup, top with the boiling water, and stir until the sugars and cocoa dissolve.

TO MAKE THE STRAWBERRY WHIPPED CREAM: Put the spiral from a Hawthorne strainer in a cocktail shaker; then combine the heavy cream and ½ ounce of strawberry syrup. Shake until you can feel the cream solidify, about 2 minutes. Top the hot chocolate with the strawberry whipped cream and garnish with a scored strawberry perched on the rim. Stir to enjoy.

Tom Trench's Tiki Tipple

YIELD: 1 DRINK

As hesitant as Katie is to share the spotlight, it seems a minor miracle Tom gets any screentime at all. Of course, the grim visage of his gas-mask head ensures Katie is the more relatable face of 666 News. With Katie taking charge, Tom presumably has plenty of time to kick back between airings with a relaxing drink, and there's little more relaxing than the tropical fruit flavors of this tiki-themed drink.

1 large mango, peeled and sliced, 2 slices reserved for garnish

½ cup coconut water

1 banana, sliced, 1 slice reserved for garnish

1 ounce orgeat

SPECIAL EQUIPMENT

Blender

In a blender, blend the mango, coconut water, half the banana, and the orgeat. Pour the mixture into a Collins glass.

On a cocktail skewer, thread 1 mango slice, 1 slice of banana, and then a final mango slice for the garnish. Place on the glass rim and serve.

THE IDEA OF LILITH

YIELD: 1 DRINK

Even though she currently resides in Hevan, Charlie's mother Lilith casts a long shadow across Pentagram City. Even absent, though, Lilith remains an inspiration to her daughter, who hopes to live up to the hopes and dreams that fueled her parent. Feel a bit of that inspiration with this fig-flavored mocktail inspired by the Queen of Hell herself.

2 ounces Black Tea & Fig "Bourbon" (page 12)

½ ounce orange juice

½ ounce grenadine

¼ ounce lemon juice

One 4-ounce King Cube

½ fresh fig

In a cocktail shaker filled with ice, combine black tea and fig "bourbon," orange juice, grenadine, and lemon juice.

Shake well; then strain over the King Cube into a rocks glass. Garnish with a skewered fig and serve.

TWO REBELLIOUS DREAMERS

YIELD: 1 DRINK

At the very beginning of creation, Lucifer and Lilith's shared independence and dreams of more led to them falling in love and rebelling against Heaven itself. Though their decision to share free will with humanity brought evil into the world and caused the creation of Hell, their dream of something better lives on through their daughter. Charlie has never forgotten her parents' story, and you can remember it, too, with this apple-flavored concoction. It probably won't unlock the forbidden knowledge of Heaven, but it'll taste good all the same!

1½ ounces Apple Shrub (page 13)

¾ ounce Honey Syrup (page 10)

½ ounce lemon juice

One 4-ounce ice sphere

1 dehydrated apple wheel

In a cocktail shaker filled with ice, add the apple shrub, honey syrup, and lemon juice and shake well.

Strain the mixture into a rocks class over the ice sphere. Garnish with the dehydrated apple wheel perched on the rim and serve.

The Hazbin

YIELD: 1 DRINK

Charlie's dream manifested, the Hazbin Hotel is where Hell's Sinners have a chance to set things right and try to become a better person. The road to redemption is a tough one, so the hotel's signature drink aims to offer a sweet treat to perk up the spirits. Coffee's a popular way to start a new day, so this drink, layered with vanilla and almond syrups, can hopefully lead to a new beginning for every resident. Probably not the top of Husk's suggested drink list, but worth giving a try all the same!

VANILLA TURMERIC FOAM

2 ounces vanilla creamer

1 dash ground turmeric

THE HAZBIN

½ ounce sweetened condensed milk

¾ ounce Vanilla Almond Syrup (page 11)

1 ounce espresso

SPECIAL EQUIPMENT

Milk frother

TO MAKE THE VANILLA TURMERIC FOAM: In a milk frother, blend the creamer and turmeric. Discard any extra foam; do not store.

TO MAKE THE HAZBIN: In a classic Manhattan glass, combine the condensed milk, vanilla almond syrup, and espresso. Top with the vanilla turmeric foam and serve.

ABEL'S OFFERING

YIELD: 2 DRINKS

Adam may have been felled in battle, but his legacy is far from forgotten (and not just because he's the Original Dick). His son Abel remains in Heaven, though he clearly lacks the cruelty and conviction of his father. Here's a slushy to match Abel's energy, with banana and guava flavors to highlight the pink and yellow of his uniform.

2 cups guava juice

1 cup papaya juice

2 ounces Brown Sugar Syrup (page 11)

8 ounces pineapple juice

SPECIAL EQUIPMENT

Slushy machine

In a slushy machine, blend the guava juice, papaya juice, and brown sugar syrup. Once the slushy forms, pour the mixture into a 6-ounce goblet or stemless wineglass and put in the freezer.

Clean the slushy machine and then blend the pineapple juice.

Remove half of the slushy from the freezer; then top with the pineapple slushy. Repeat with a second glass. Stir to enjoy.

A Sip of Speaker

YIELD: 1 DRINK

Though Sera leads the seraphim, there are forces above even her in Heaven. Serving as the voice of God, the Speaker offers guidance to the seraphim as the conflict with Hell intensifies. With a gold-flake garnish to represent a transcendent pedigree, this flavored drink captures the shining aura of the Speaker.

- One 4-ounce King Cube
- 4 ounces soda water
- 1½ ounces Ginger Syrup (page 11)
- ½ lemon
- 1 pinch edible gold flakes

Put the King Cube in a rocks glass. Pour in the soda water and ginger syrup.

Squeeze the lemon over the top. Stir gently and garnish with the gold flakes before serving.

2

C~~M~~OCKTAILS for Bad Boys!!

Angel's Fave

YIELD: 1 DRINK

Angel Dust is one of Hell's top porn stars, and he's happy to prove it at the drop of a hat. Or, preferably, the drop of someone's pants. A drink for all of Angel's blunt come-ons and on-the-nose innuendos, what else could it be but a classic porn star martini? Reflective of Angel's own journey of growth and redemption, this drink can be enjoyed with or without alcohol. Whatever your persuasion, enjoy a nice, big gulp of Angel's passion . . . fruit-flavored drink.

1½ ounces vodka

2 ounces passion fruit juice

1 ounce filtered water

¾ ounce Brown Sugar Syrup (page 11)

¼ ounce lime juice

1 dash vanilla extract

1 dash white cocktail glitter

In a cocktail shaker filled with ice, add the passion fruit juice, vodka, water, brown sugar syrup, lime juice, vanilla, and white cocktail glitter and shake well.

Strain into a coupe glass and serve.

for Bad Boys!!

SIR PENTIOUS'S SACRIFICE

YIELD: 1 DRINK

Though he first came to the hotel as an undercover agent of the Vees, no resident better embodies the spirit of Charlie's mission than Sir Pentious. In the final battle against Adam, Pentious gave his afterlife to try to protect his friends from the exorcists, an act that would ultimately see him ascend to Heaven. Remember that sacrifice with this mocktail, vanilla ice cream floating to the top like the fluffy, white clouds Pentious finds himself residing upon. And don't forget his Hellish origins with an alternate cocktail version.

3 small to medium scoops vanilla ice cream

½ teaspoon chocolate syrup

9 ounces Guinness 0 or Guinness

Put the ice-cream scoops in a pint glass; then slowly pour in the Guinness 0. or Guinness

Drizzle with the chocolate syrup and serve.

for Bad Boys!!

CHERRI BOMB

YIELD: 1 DRINK

Cherri Bomb lives up to her name when she arrives at the Hazbin Hotel, doing her best to blow up all of Angel's progress on their night out. And though she'd much rather keep kicking back and enjoying hard drinks like this cherry-flavored cocktail, this drink can easily be made into a mocktail version for a more *responsible* kind of night. It's harder to fit a bomb into a drink, but you can bet the popping candy on the rim will have your taste buds blowing up with flavor!

1 lemon wedge, scored

½ packet cherry-flavored popping candy

6 maraschino cherries, divided

¾ teaspoon maraschino cherry syrup

6 ounces Mexican Coca-Cola

2 OUNCES BOURBON

Run the lemon wedge around half the rim of a Collins glass, dipping the glass in the popping candy to coat the rim. Discard the lemon.

Add three cherries and the cherry syrup to the glass and muddle lightly. Add the ice, Coca-Cola, AND BOURBON and stir gently.

Coat the remaining three cherries in the Pop Rocks, skewer for garnish, and serve.

KeeKee's Dish

YIELD: 1 DRINK

KeeKee pulls double duty as both Charlie's pet and the physical embodiment of the hotel itself. Whether she's comforting Charlie in the aftermath of an extermination or helping rebuild the hotel following the battle with the exorcists, KeeKee always shifts her shape to fit the mood. Like this beverage, she's truly the cat's pajamas. And, like KeeKee, your drink can shape-shift, too, with both alcoholic and nonalcoholic options!

TURMERIC AND GINGER ICE

½ cup filtered water

3 lemons, peeled and quartered

1 lemon, quartered, skin on

2½-inch piece fresh ginger, skin on and coarsely chopped

1-inch fresh turmeric root, peeled and coarsely chopped

GOLD KEY-SHAPED ICE

¼ cup filtered water

1 pinch gold cocktail glitter

1 pinch edible gold flakes

KEEKEE'S DISH

2 ounces NA "Gin" (page 12)

or 2 ounces Old Tom gin

¾ ounce lemon juice

¾ ounce Honey Syrup (page 10)

2 ounces soda water, divided (optional)

TO MAKE THE TURMERIC AND GINGER ICE: In a blender, combine the water, lemons, ginger, and turmeric root and blend for 2 minutes. Strain the mixture through a fine-mesh strainer. Pour the mixture into an ice-cube tray and let freeze overnight.

TO MAKE THE GOLD KEY-SHAPED ICE: In a liquid measuring cup, combine the water and gold cocktail glitter and stir well. Pour the mixture into a small (½ to 1 ounce) key-shaped mold. Add the gold flakes on top. Allow to freeze through.

TO MAKE KEEKEE'S DISH: In a cocktail shaker filled with ice, add the NA "gin," lemon juice, and honey syrup. Shake and strain the mixture into a short glass (such as a rocks glass) over a few fresh ice cubes and the turmeric and ginger ice cube. Top with key-shaped gold ice.

or 2 ounces Old Tom gin

As the ice melts, the color will change to a yellowy-orange, and the gold flakes and cocktail glitter will combine with the drink. Add 1 ounce of soda water at a time to balance the flavors of the turmeric and ginger ice cube as it melts.

for Bad Boys!!

Lute's Revenge

YIELD: 1 DRINK

There's no bigger hater of the damned than Lute, an exorcist with a megalomaniacal desire to exterminate fallen souls. She's got a special hatred for Vaggie, whom she sees as a traitor to Heaven and everything the exorcists stand for. Their bitter rivalry comes to head during the battle at the hotel, and this mocktail captures that bitterness perfectly. Of course, feel free to make an alcoholic version instead; no doubt Lute needed a stiff drink after losing her arm.

1½ ounces NA "Gin" (page 12)

1½ ounces Ghia Original Aperitif

¾ ounce Ghia Berry Aperitif

¾ ounce Simple Syrup (page 10)

½ ounce lemon juice

One 4-ounce ice sphere

1 pinch edible gold flakes

or 1½ ounces London dry-style gin

In a cocktail shaker filled with ice, add the NA "gin," Ghia Aperitif Original, Ghia Aperitif Berry, simple syrup, and lemon juice. Shake and then strain the mixture over the ice sphere into a wineglass. Garnish with gold flakes and serve.

or 1½ ounces London dry-style gin

SERA OFF DUTY

YIELD: 12 DRINKS

As one of the seraphim leading Heaven, Sera knows how to put on a good face publicly while getting the dirty work done in secret. Though Sera plays at being sympathetic to Charlie's efforts, she was the one to first sanction the exterminations in Hell, a secret she's none too happy to see come out during Charlie's visit to Heaven. Sangrita is a sweet drink, matching the persona Sera likes to show to the world, but it's also Spanish for "little blood," something Sera has plenty of on her hands. Like Sera, you can enjoy a mocktail version if you're putting on a squeaky-clean public image, or add in some tequila to take the edge off after a rough day.

6 ounces tomato juice
4 ounces orange juice
4 ounces pomegranate juice
2 ounces lime juice
1 ounce pineapple juice
1 ounce Brown Sugar Syrup (page 11)
1 ounce Simple Syrup (page 10)
1 teaspoon salt
1 tablespoon Tajín, divided
12 lime wedges, scored
72 ounces soda water (6 ounces per NA drink)
12 ounces tequila

In a pitcher, combine the tomato, orange, pomegranate, lime, and pineapple juices with the brown sugar syrup, simple syrup, salt, and half the Tajín. Stir well. Pour the remaining Tajín onto a plate.

Run a lime wedge around a Collins glass and dip the glass in Tajín to coat the rim; then add ice and 2 ounces of the sangrita, topped with 6 ounces of soda water. Use the lime wedge as garnish for the rim of the glass. Repeat for the remaining drinks.

Store the sangrita in a sealed container in the refrigerator for up to 1 week.

Serve as a shot in a Tajín-rimmed shot glass alongside a shot of tequila!

The Bloody Overlords

YIELD: 1 DRINK

Hell may be a chaotic place, but you can be sure it'd be even more unruly without the Overlords to keep their fellow Sinners in line. From the media empire of the Vees to Rosie's commanding grip over Cannibal Town, the Overlords all wield their power differently, but all in service of keeping themselves at the top of the food chain. Spicy, bloody, and served with an over-the-top garnish, this drink that can be made with either alcoholic or nonalcoholic beer captures all the grandeur and self-aggrandizing of being one of Hell's Overlords.

1 lime wedge, scored

1 tablespoon Tajín, sprinkled on a plate

2 ounces Bloody Mary mix

8 ounces NA Mexican lager
or Mexican lager

GARNISH

1 pickled jalapeño

1 ounce Oaxacan cheese

Run the lime wedge halfway around the rim of a Collins glass and dip the glass in the Tajín to coat the rim. Put about three ice cubes in the glass, the Bloody Mary mix, and then top off with the NA Mexican lager.
or Mexican lager

TO MAKE THE GARNISH: Cut open the jalapeño and stuff it with the cheese. Grill the stuffed pepper over medium heat until the cheese melts and the jalapeño shows grill marks (about 5 minutes).

Garnish with the grilled and Oaxacan cheese–stuffed pickled jalapeño and serve.

I Nearly Scrambled Myself

YIELD: 1 DRINK

What would Sir Pentious do without his loyal, lovable Egg Boiz by his side? Like the snake they serve, the Egg Boiz might not be the most competent, but they get by with plenty of charm and a general lack of threat. With this egg white drink, you can avoid having to scramble any of those adorable minions and simply enjoy a sip with or without rum while you ponder if bank accounts really are a scam created by the shadow government.

or 2 ounces white rum

- 2 ounces filtered water
- ½ ounce lemon juice
- ½ ounce Ginger Syrup (page 11)
- ½ ounce Brown Sugar Syrup (page 11)
- 1 egg white
- 2 candy eyes

In a cocktail shaker with one ice cube, add the water, lemon juice, ginger syrup, brown sugar syrup, and egg white.

or rum

Shake until you can't hear the ice cube anymore; then add more ice and shake again for about 2 minutes.

Strain into a rocks glass. Gently place the candy eyes on top of the egg-white foam for garnish.

for Bad Boys!!

REEE-SPONSIBLE NIGHT ON THE TOWN!

YIELD: 4 DRINKS

When Charlie and Vaggie head to Heaven for their meeting with Sera, Charlie feels confident she can trust the other residents—and a visiting Cherri Bomb—to keep on the straight and narrow while she's away. Of course, temptation is around every corner in Hell, but Charlie knows she can count on her crew to do the right thing. Here's an innocent batch of punch for everyone to enjoy while they make good choices. If you end up choosing to spike that punch, well, hey, I'm sure you'll still drink responsibly!

1 cup pomegranate juice
½ cup tart cherry juice
½ cup pineapple juice
½ cup lemon juice
½ cup Simple Syrup (page 10)
12 maraschino cherries

4 ounces white rum
¾ ounce banana liqueur
12 dehydrated banana wheels

In a large pitcher, combine the pomegranate, cherry, and pineapple juices and simple syrup.

THEN ADD THE RUM AND BANANA LIQUEUR!

Add one ice cube and stir until the ice cube starts to melt.

Pour over fresh ice cubes into a rocks glass. Garnish each drink with three skewered cherries.

Or add three skewered banana wheels!

The Apple Doesn't Fall Far

YIELD: 1 DRINK

Early on, it's clear that Lucifer's past dealings with Heaven have left him scared to stand up for himself or his subjects. In reuniting with his daughter, though, Lucifer rediscovers the rebellious spirit that first led him to Hell. In the end, he stands with Charlie in the battle against the exorcists, proving that the apple hasn't fallen far from the tree of knowledge. The sweet nature of their relationship is captured by this apple shrub mocktail, whereas the added burn of some applejack whiskey can reflect the tough times between daughter and absentee father.

1-inch piece peeled ginger plus 3 slices for garnish

1 ounce Apple Shrub (page 13)

½ ounce Agave Syrup (page 11)

1 lemon wheel, halved

½ cup boiling water (212°F)

2 dehydrated apple wheels

1 ounce applejack whiskey

In a mug, put the ginger, chopped into wheels, and then add the apple shrub and agave syrup.

Express the lemon wheel slices into the mug, top with the water, and stir.

Add the applejack whiskey and stir.

Skewer one of the remaining ginger wheels; then run the skewer through one dehydrated apple wheel; repeat the pattern and garnish.

Yum Blood

YIELD: 1 DRINK

When it comes to Cannibal Town, the rosy—and Rosie—exterior can only go so far in hiding the inherent violence of its cannibalistic residents. Sure, there's plenty of smiling faces and a nice, fruity drink on offer, but can you really be sure that dark, thick liquid is just a mix of blueberries and black currant? You can take it straight up, or you can add some bourbon to help it go down easy; either way, you're just going to have to take these flesh-eaters at their word that Yum Blood is just a name.

¼ cup fresh blackberries, plus 3 blackberries for garnish

2 ounces Black Currant "Bourbon" (page 13)

¾ ounce lemon juice

½ ounce Simple Syrup (page 10)

1 ounce bourbon

In a cocktail shaker, muddle the blackberries.

Add ice, black currant "bourbon," lemon juice, and simple syrup.

Add the bourbon!

Shake and strain into a coupe glass.

Garnish with three skewered blackberries.

A Happy Day in Hell

YIELD: 1 DRINK

Even in the aftermath of an extermination, Charlie's spirit and dreams of redemption remain indomitable. She has so much confidence in her plans, she bursts into song as she heads for her meeting with Adam, letting her optimism flow into the streets of a Hell that'll hopefully be happy sooner than later. In honor of her dream, enjoy this light, fruity mocktail. If you're feeling particularly hellish, add the optional flaming rum element. Happy or not, it's still Hell, after all.

2 ounces NA "Vodka" (page 12)

1 ounce Raspberry Syrup (page 11)

½ ounce lemon juice

One 4-ounce King Cube

1/2 ounce overproof rum

1/2 lime, hollowed out

SPECIAL EQUIPMENT

1 match or lighter (optional)

In a cocktail shaker filled with ice, add the NA "vodka," raspberry syrup, and lemon juice and shake well. Strain over the King Cube into a rocks glass.

Add the rum to a hollowed-out lime half and use a match or lighter to set it alight! Extinguish the flame. Pour the rum into the cocktail and enjoy.

Virgin Sacrifice Piña Coladas

YIELD: 1 DRINK

Hell's a cruel place where even the allegedly innocent can find themselves trapped in its fiery embrace. There's no virgin sacrifice required to enjoy this Piña Colada, and there's also no need to enjoy the virgin version of it if you'd like to add a bit of white rum to the mixture.

½ cup coconut water

½ cup frozen pineapple chunks

1 ounce strawberry jam or jelly

1½ ounces Coco Lopez

1½ ounces pineapple juice

2 ounces white rum

1 teaspoon strawberry syrup

SPECIAL EQUIPMENT

Blender

Hurricane glass

In a blender, combine the coconut water, frozen pineapple chunks, strawberry jam, Coco Lopez, and pineapple juice.

Add the rum!

Blend until smooth. Dip a hurricane glass in the strawberry syrup to rim the glass. Pour the mocktail or cocktail from the blender into the glass and serve.

for Bad Boys!!

3

~~MOCKTAILS~~ Cocktails for Boozers!!!

Beelzejuice

YIELD: 1 DRINK

There are few things Sinners and Hellborns love more than getting their drink on, so it's no surprise that Hell has more than a few favorite cocktails. With Beelzejuice, you can enjoy a hellish, honey-flavored take on a classic Manhattan and drink like the damned! Be sure to drink responsibly and remember to keep the party's tasty energy sweet and not sour.

- 2 ounces bourbon
- ¾ ounce Bénédictine
- ¼ ounce Honey Syrup (page 10)
- 1 maraschino cherry

In a mixing glass filled with ice, add the bourbon, Bénédictine, and honey syrup. Stir.

Strain into a martini glass and drop the cherry into the drink for garnish.

SSSSIR PENTIOUS

YIELD: 1 DRINK

Sir Pentious's crush on Cherri Bomb makes itself painfully obvious during the crew's night out with the chaotic explosives expert. His aborted attempts at flirting lead to all manner of problems for Pentious, including a promise to buy drinks for *everybody* in the bar! Maybe a bit more liquid courage could've helped the Victorian-era viper speak his mind, though this absinthe-based cocktail may have just knocked him flat instead.

1½ ounces rye

½ ounce sweet vermouth

¼ ounce absinthe

¼ ounce Bénédictine

2 dashes Angostura bitters

1 lemon swath

In a mixing glass filled with ice, add the rye, vermouth, absinthe, Bénédictine, and bitters.

Stir well. Strain into a classic Manhattan glass or martini glass.

Express the lemon swath over the glass and discard it before serving.

LUCIFER THE DREAMER

YIELD: 1 DRINK

From his initial rebellious streak that got him cast out of Heaven to his support of Charlie's mission, nothing's ever fully gotten rid of Lucifer's dreamer spirit. In honor of that optimism, here's a strong cocktail for the strongest angel in Hell. Be sure to include those gummy snakes to capture not only Lucifer's serpentlike seduction, but as a reminder of just how ostentatious and showy the King of Hell can be.

1½ ounces rye whiskey

¾ ounce applejack whiskey

¾ ounce Brovo Uncharted Rhapsody American Forest Liqueur

2 dashes Amargo Chuncho bitters

1 twin snake gummy candy

SPECIAL EQUIPMENT

1 match or lighter

In a mixing glass filled with ice, add the rye, applejack, Brovo, and bitters. Stir.

Slide the gummy around the base of a classic Manhattan glass. Ignite the match or lighter and slightly melt the back of the heads of the snakes, pressing them firmly to the stem so they stick, face up, as if they're climbing the stem.

Strain the drink into the glass and serve.

ALASTOR'S MANTRA

YIELD: 1 DRINK

There's no telling what Alastor has planned at any minute, and that's just the way he likes it. However good or bad the situation, he makes sure to keep his cool and a smile on his face. As he tells Charlie, a smile can keep your enemies guessing, and it's clear Alastor has plenty of those. Whatever happens, Alastor intends to keep on grinning, so here's a cocktail to go along with all the best laid plans of mice and Sinners.

- ¾ ounce London dry-style gin
- ¾ ounce Dolin Génépy des Alpes
- ½ ounce Simple Syrup (page 10)
- ½ ounce Bitter Bianca
- ½ ounce lemon juice
- 1 barspoon maraschino cherry syrup

In a cocktail shaker filled with ice, add the gin, Génépy des Alpes, simple syrup, Bitter Bianca, and lemon juice. Shake well.

Add the cherry syrup to a Nick & Nora glass.

Gently pour the cocktail into the glass at an angle, so as not to disturb the cherry syrup.

Sip as is or stir for a more . . . bloody look.

VOLUME

Whiskers's Sour

YIELD: 1 DRINK

Nobody appreciates a good cocktail like the Hazbin Hotel's resident bartender! Well, okay, Husk's not that picky, given that most of the time he's happy to just throw back whatever bottle of booze is closest. But he got the job for a reason—contract with Alastor notwithstanding—so here's the sort of high-end cocktail you could probably order from the miffed mixologist on a good day. A classic whiskey sour! Or, as Angel Dust might call it, a Whiskers Sour.

2 ounces bourbon

¾ ounce Simple Syrup (page 10)

½ ounce lime juice

½ ounce lemon juice

1 egg white

1 maraschino cherry

1 lemon wheel

4 dashes Angostura bitters

In a cocktail shaker containing one ice cube, add the bourbon, simple syrup, lime and lemon juice, and egg white. Shake until you can't hear the ice anymore, then add more ice.

Shake for about 2 minutes more, then strain into a rocks glass.

Garnish with a skewered cherry and lemon wheel and generously dash with Angostura bitters.

The Vees

YIELD: 1 DRINK

None of Hell's Overlords are quite as in-your-face and ostentatious as the Vees. From brainwashing users of VoxTek electronics to keeping the horniest Sinners begging for more, the Vees have a controlling interest in favorite vices of the damned. What better way to represent this terrible trio than a layered shot of three different liqueurs? Just don't let Velvette make it for you . . .

½ ounce espresso liqueur

½ ounce ube cream liqueur

½ ounce orange liqueur (Cointreau recommended)

Put each bottle of alcohol in the freezer for 30 minutes to an hour.

Placing a barspoon upside down in a shot glass, gently pour the espresso liqueur over it into the bottom of the glass.

Repeat with the ube liqueur and the orange liqueur to create layers.

Stir when ready to enjoy.

Mimzy's Bee's Knees

YIELD: 1 DRINK

This unflappable flapper brings a whole heap of trouble to the hotel when she first swings by, counting on her old pal Alastor to clean up her mess. Her visit is brief, but it's clear she's got plenty of history with an unappreciative Husk. As such, he's likely made her an era-appropriate drink at least once or twice over the years. Enjoy a drink that roars like the Twenties with this Prohibition-era Bee's Knees cocktail!

1½ ounces London dry-style gin

¾ ounce lemon juice

¾ ounce Cinnamon Honey Syrup (page 11)

1 cinnamon stick

SPECIAL EQUIPMENT

1 match or lighter

In a cocktail shaker filled with ice, add the gin, lemon juice, and cinnamon-honey syrup. Shake and strain into a coupe glass. Ignite the cinnamon stick and then extinguish it, placing the smoking end sticking out of the drink.

Razzle and/or Dazzle

Yield: 2 shots

Most of the time, Charlie's pet dragons are the picture of adorableness in their little tuxedo jackets. When it's time to throw down, though, they can rely on their full demon forms to take on whatever threat has shown up at the hotel's doors. These paired shots capture both of the pair's moods: a sweet concoction for pet mode and a flaming shot for when things get a bit spicier.

RAZZLE

½ ounce pineapple rum

½ ounce lime juice

¼ ounce Aperol

¼ ounce Simple Syrup (page 10)

DAZZLE

1½ ounces Dolin Génépy des Alpes or Green Chartreuse

SPECIAL EQUIPMENT

1 match or lighter

TO MAKE THE RAZZLE SHOT: In a cocktail shaker filled with ice, add the pineapple rum, lime juice, Aperol, and simple syrup. Shake well. Strain into a shot glass.

TO MAKE THE DAZZLE SHOT: Pour the Génépy des Alpes into a shot glass, then ignite with match or lighter. Extinguish before enjoying. The Dazzle goes well with the Razzle as a chaser.

Lilith on the Beach

YIELD: 1 DRINK

While her husband and daughter have struggled down in Hell, Lilith's spent several years secreted away in Heaven, spending at least some of that time lounging by the beach. Though Lute tries to make it clear her vacation is over, you can enjoy some of that Heavenly relaxation with this medley of fruity flavors in this elevated take on a classic Sex on the Beach.

1½ ounces mezcal

1½ ounces orange juice

1 ounce cranberry liqueur

½ ounce peach schnapps

½ ounce Simple Syrup (page 10)

1 pinch salt

One 4-ounce King Cube

1 dehydrated blood orange wheel

1 maraschino cherry

In a cocktail shaker filled with ice, add the mezcal, orange juice, cranberry liqueur, peach schnapps, simple syrup, and salt.

Shake well and then strain over the King Cube. Skewer the orange wheel and the cherry to garnish before serving.

ZESTIAL'S FLIP

YIELD: 1 DRINK

Like his fellow Overlord Alastor, Zestial strikes fear into the hearts of any other demon that dares to cross his path. Hell, most demons would rather self-immolate than even risk it! It's clear that despite his calm demeanor, Zestial can flip the switch in an instant when provoked. For one of Hell's most ancient demons, here's a take on one of the oldest cocktails around—a rum flip, garnished with a blackberry spider to honor the demon himself.

2 ounces sherry-cask-aged rum

1½ ounces Blackberry Syrup (page 11)

¾ ounce lemon juice

1 egg

¼ ounce pastis or absinthe

1 fresh blackberry

8 strings black shoestring licorice

SPECIAL EQUIPMENT

1 skewer

In a cocktail shaker with one ice cube, add the rum, blackberry syrup, pastis or absinthe, lemon juice, and egg. Shake until you can't hear the ice anymore.

Add more ice and shake vigorously. The shaker will frost up; keep shaking for a few seconds beyond that.

Strain over two or three fresh ice cubes into a Collins glass.

Poke 4 shallow holes in the blackberry along each side, then push the licorice strings into each hole to create the "spider legs."

Garnish with a skewered blackberry spider.

Meistro's Chorus

YIELD: 1 DRINK

Meistro's formal look might suggest a bit of class, but this demon has a habit of getting right into the mess of his fellow Overlords, as he is all too happy to keep tabs on Alastor and dish with fellow Overlord Zeezi. With this flaming-blue drink, you can enjoy the spirit of Meistro the next time you share drinks and the latest gossip with your own friends.

1 kiwi, halved

1 ounce white rum

¾ ounce lime juice

½ ounce Velvet Falernum

½ ounce orgeat

¼ ounce blue curaçao

¼ ounce overproof rum

SPECIAL EQUIPMENT

1 match or lighter

Core one half of the kiwi so that only the shell remains, leaving enough fruit to support the thin skin of the kiwi. Peel, then muddle the other half in a cocktail shaker. Add ice, then the rum, lime juice, Velvet Falernum, orgeat, and blue curaçao. Shake well.

Pour into a goblet or stemless wineglass and add ice to fill the glass.

Top with the hollowed-out kiwi, fill with overproof rum, and ignite. Extinguish the flame and pour the shot into the cocktail for a stronger drink or discard.

UGH, SUSAN

YIELD: 1 DRINK

Opinionated and in-your-face, Susan gives Charlie nothing but grief when she tries to rally the residents to fight against the exorcists. Still, despite her surliness, she inadvertently helps inspire Charlie to harness her leadership skills and rally the cannibal forces, so she's not all bad . . . well, as far as cannibals go. This floral cocktail captures the rosy exterior of Cannibal Town while also providing a bit of bitterness for the most cantankerous cannibal around.

2 ounces bourbon

2 ounces Lo-Fi Gentian Amaro

2 dashes rose water

Pinch dehydrated or fresh edible rose petals

In a mixing glass filled with ice, add the bourbon, Amaro, and rose water. Stir and strain into a Nick & Nora glass. Garnish with the rose petals floating on top before serving.

CONSENT

YIELD: 2 CUPS GELATIN DESSERT

When the residents of the hotel head out for a night on the town with Cherri Bomb, they certainly know how to have a good time! And, as this club's name suggests, there's no having a good time without consent all around. It's also fun to order a round of shots—ideally for everyone!—so be sure to enjoy these cherry Jell-O shots before you let your carnal impulses take over.

1 cup white rum

1 cup boiling filtered water (212°F)

1 box black cherry Jell-O

1 lemon or lime wedge, scored

2 tablespoons powdered sugar

Combine the rum, boiling water, and Jell-O and stir until the gelatin is fully dissolved.

Pour into shot glasses and refrigerate overnight.

Once the shots have solidified, run the citrus wedge along the rim of each glass, dipping them in powdered sugar to garnish.

Radio Killed the Video Star

YIELD: 1 DRINK

When Vox senses a power vacuum, he's quick to try to fill it with a commanding broadcast. Of course, his long-standing rivalry with Alastor leaves him with one old-timey signal he can't quite overcome. This scotch-based drink for the leader of the Vees is plenty strong . . . though maybe not strong enough to overwhelm the Radio Demon.

2 ounces Scotch

1 ounce sweet vermouth

½ ounce maple syrup

One 4-ounce King Cube

1 orange swath

SPECIAL EQUIPMENT

1 match

In a mixing glass filled with ice, add the Scotch, vermouth, and maple syrup. Stir and strain over the King Cube into a rocks glass.

Light a match and hold it over the drink; express the orange swath over the flame. Discard the match and orange swath and serve.

THE DEAD EXORCIST

YIELD: 1 DRINK

When Velvette tosses the severed angel head onto the Overlord meeting table, we get a look at the gold blood that runs through their veins. Though the cannibal crowd would probably be happy to take a drink straight from the source, this cocktail re-creates that golden glow in a more palatable form. Enjoy an added hint of absinthe to raise you up to the heavens above.

1½ ounces absinthe

¾ ounce Bénédictine

4 ounces soda water

In a Collins glass, combine the absinthe and Bénédictine; then add enough ice to fill the glass.

Top with soda water, stir gently, and serve.

Something Strong

YIELD: 1 DRINK

Though Angel and Husk start out at each other's throats, the lovable losers eventually find common ground through their mutual servitude to abusive Overlords. Husk might begrudgingly admit he's made any friends in the hotel, but that doesn't mean he won't make Angel a strong drink after a rough day at the studio. Relax after a hard day—or long night—of your own with this take on a classic corpse reviver.

¾ ounce London dry-style gin

¾ ounce Aperol

¾ ounce Lillet Blanc

¾ ounce lemon juice

½ ounce Simple Syrup (page 10)

1 lemon wheel

In a cocktail shaker filled with ice, add the gin, Aperol, Lillet Blanc, lemon juice, and simple syrup.

Shake well and strain into a martini glass. Add the lemon wheel to the rim of the glass to garnish.

Poison

YIELD: 1 DRINK

One of Angel Dust's biggest struggles is with the abusive relationship he has with his boss Valentino. He compares this relationship to an addiction, likening it to a poison he can't quit. This strong cocktail can hopefully serve as an escape from the toxicity, the sort that might take the edge off after a tense day.

2 ounces bourbon

¾ ounce Amaro Averna

3 dashes whiskey-barrel-aged bitters

1 maraschino cherry

In a mixing glass filled with ice, add the bourbon, Amaro Averna, and bitters.

Stir and strain into a classic Manhattan glass. Garnish with a skewered cherry.

Baxter's Bad Batch

YIELD: 1 DRINK

With a win against the exorcists, the hotel manages to expand and attract new guests. That includes this marine mad scientist with an antisocial bent. And though he has a knack for invention and troublemaking, the last thing you want to assume is that he's the hotel's new Pentious. Enjoy a bit of what sets Baxter apart with the saltwater flavors of seaweed and oyster in this cocktail.

2 ounces Seaweed-Infused Gin (page 13)

2 ounces Cocchi Americano

1 raw oyster

In a mixing glass filled with ice, add the seaweed-infused gin and Cocchi Americano.

Stir and strain into a martini glass. Garnish with an oyster on the rim to enjoy as a chaser!

THE HAZBIN'S NEW LOOK

YIELD: 1 DRINK

The battle with the exorcists left the hotel in a rough state, but fortunately, that breakdown was the basis for a stellar glow-up. With a dash of activated charcoal to capture the fire-and-brimstone magic that made this makeover possible, here's a jet-black drink with a hint of gold to capture the brand-new look of the Hazbin Hotel.

- ¾ ounce mezcal
- ¾ ounce reposado tequila
- ½ ounce Aperol
- ½ ounce sweet vermouth
- 1 dash activated charcoal
- 1 dash gold cocktail glitter

In a mixing glass filled with ice, add the mezcal, tequila, Aperol, vermouth, activated charcoal, and cocktail glitter. Stir well.

Pour into a martini glass and serve.

MANEATER GIMLET

YIELD: 1 DRINK

In addition to running Cannibal Town, Rosie has her emporium sell all manner of merchandising to the residents; like any good Overlord, she knows the importance of diversifying her portfolio. Enjoy a drink from Rosie's personal collection with this take on a gin gimlet. Be sure to mind the hot sauce lurking under the surface, the same way you'd need to be mindful of a seemingly charming cannibal.

2 ounces London dry-style gin

¾ ounce lime juice

½ ounce Simple Syrup (page 10)

Must be Rosie's Maneater Gin!

5 dashes cayenne pepper hot sauce

1 dehydrated red chile pepper

In a cocktail shaker filled with ice, add the gin, lime juice, simple syrup, and hot sauce. Shake well.

Strain into a coupe glass; then drop the dehydrated chile pepper into the glass for garnish.

Love in a Bottle

YIELD: 2 DRINKS

Husk takes a while to open up to the other residents of the hotel, and even then, he does so begrudgingly. However, Husk never has an issue opening up a bottle, and he may have no greater love than whatever hard liquor he's currently in the process of throwing back. Get a drink that makes you as happy as it does Husk with this glittering vodka cocktail.

- 3 ounces Hibiscus Vodka (page 13)
- 1½ ounces lime juice
- 1½ ounces Simple Syrup (page 10)
- ½ barspoon red cocktail glitter

In a cocktail shaker filled with ice, add the hibiscus vodka, lime juice, simple syrup, and cocktail glitter. Shake well.

Strain into an empty glass bottle and serve alongside two classic Manhattan or martini glasses.

HARDER DADDY

YIELD: 1 DRINK

There's no choosing words carefully around Angel Dust, as he'll find a way to turn just about any turn of phrase into an innuendo. Better to just lean in and embrace your mind's dirtiest impulses. With the Harder Daddy cocktail, you can enjoy a watermelon-infused drink that would make Angel proud . . . and probably make Husk roll his eyes at you for ordering one.

½ cup cubes fresh watermelon

1½ ounces white rum

¾ ounce orgeat

½ ounce lime juice

1 large slice watermelon, about 1-inch thick

SPECIAL EQUIPMENT

1 heart-shaped cookie cutter

1 skewer

In a cocktail shaker, muddle the watermelon cubes and then add ice.

Add the rum, orgeat, and lime juice. Shake and double strain into a coupe or martini glass.

Using a heart-shaped cookie cutter, cut a heart out of the watermelon slice.

Garnish with a skewered heart-shaped watermelon wedge.

Torment & Tonic

YIELD: 1 DRINK

Charlie does her best to make Hell . . . well, not necessarily a fun place, but a tolerable one. Still, even the best day among the damned is still full of torture and torment, and that's just a fact of death. Let that hard truth wash over you with this highball, garnished with a lemon twist to capture the sour punch of the afterlife.

- 2 ounces Empress Indigo Gin
- 6 ounces tonic water
- 1 long lemon twist

In a Collins glass filled with ice, add the gin and top with the tonic water. Garnish with the lemon twist and serve.

VOX POPULI

YIELD: 1 DRINK

Early on, Vox's television empire is built on keeping the masses of Hell locked in on whatever mindless entertainment and product placement will fill the Vees' pockets the fastest. Eventually, though, he sets his sights on amassing even more power through his hypnotic broadcasts, causing trouble for Charlie and the hotel. With light-up ice cubes to capture the ethereal glow of a screen, here's a blue drink for the blue-screen face of Hell himself.

2 ounces white rum

1 ounce Simple Syrup (page 10)

¾ ounce lime juice

½ ounce blue curaçao

SPECIAL EQUIPMENT

3 light-up blue ice cubes

In a cocktail shaker filled with ice, add the white rum, simple syrup, lime juice, and blue curaçao. Shake well.

In a rocks glass, add one light-up blue ice cube and regular ice. Repeat the pattern to spread out the light-up ice cubes.

Pour the cocktail over the ice cubes and watch the blue cubes light up as they make contact with the liquid.

Love Potion

YIELD: 1 DRINK

Vox's rise to power is a team effort, with each of the Vees making new moves to cement their influence over the underworld. For Velvette, that includes a new love potion for the forlorn. Get a taste of Velvette's personal stock with this strawberry cosmo, garnished with a skull for all the sorry souls trapped under the influence of the Vees.

1 lemon swath

4 small or 3 large fresh strawberries, hulled and sliced, reserving 1 slice for garnish

1½ ounces vodka

¾ ounce lemon juice

¾ ounce Simple Syrup (page 10)

SPECIAL EQUIPMENT

Kitchen scissors

Using kitchen scissors and a sharp knife, cut the lemon swath into a skull shape. Set aside.

In a cocktail shaker, muddle the strawberries.

Add ice, vodka, lemon juice, and simple syrup to the cocktail shaker.

Shake and double-strain into a coupe or martini glass.

Garnish with the strawberry slice skewered under the skull-shaped lemon swath.

4

ROOM SERVICE for Gluttons!!!!

Niffty's Favorite Snack

V ♥ YIELD: 1 SMALL BOWL OF GUACAMOLE (ABOUT 1/2 CUP)

Niffty may be the hotel's most unhinged resident, but there's no arguing that she does a great job keeping the place clean. That includes staying on top of the hotel's bug problem, one violent stabbing at a time. Here's a snack to enjoy when you take a break from cleaning up, with bug-shaped veggies to emulate the violent tendencies of Hell's best maid.

GUACAMOLE

1 small to medium avocado

¼ cup plain Greek yogurt

1 lime wedge

1 tablespoon chopped cilantro, divided

Salt

Freshly ground black pepper

BUG-SHAPED CHIPS

6 large flour tortillas

1 tablespoon olive oil

1 pinch salt

SPECIAL EQUIPMENT

Bug-shaped cookie cutters

Air fryer

TO MAKE THE GUACAMOLE: Using a fork or potato masher, mash the avocado to the desired consistency. Mix the avocado with the yogurt, squeeze the lime wedge over the top, and add ¾ tablespoon of cilantro, reserving the rest for garnish. Season to taste with salt and pepper and mix again. Garnish with the remaining ¼ tablespoon of cilantro. Serve with homemade bug-shaped chips.

TO MAKE THE BUG-SHAPED CHIPS: Preheat an air fryer to 350°F. Layer the tortillas on top of each other in two piles of three tortillas. Using a bug-shaped cookie-cutter, press firmly on the piles of tortillas, creating as many bug shapes as you can. Discard the excess tortillas and split the stacked tortillas. Brush each bug shape with olive oil and season with salt. Cook the chips in the air fryer, being careful to keep them from touching, for about 3 minutes, or until they reach the desired crispiness.

Fat Nuggets

DF ♥ YIELD: 16 SERVINGS

Though Angel is slow to open up to the other residents of the hotel, he has at least one confidant in the form of his pet pig Fat Nuggets. Angel's porky pal is there for him to snuggle up with after all the hard days and hard-partying nights. Snacking on Fat Nuggets is of course off-limits, but you can wrap up your own pigs in blankets with this appetizing finger-food classic.

2 tubes ready-made crescent rolls

One 14-ounce package cocktail franks

1 egg, whisked

Salt

Freshly ground black pepper

2 tablespoons sriracha

2 tablespoons Kewpie mayonnaise

SPECIAL EQUIPMENT

Air fryer

Preheat the air fryer to 350°F.

Cut the crescent rolls in half, maintaining their triangular shape. Wrap one cocktail frank in each triangle. Brush the tops with the egg wash and season with salt to taste. Cook in the air fryer for 3 to 4 minutes, until flaky and browned.

Meanwhile, in a small bowl, combine the sriracha and mayonnaise and season the mixture with salt and pepper to taste. For more heat, add more sriracha!

Deviled Egg Boiz

V, GF, DF ♥ YIELD: 12

When Sir Pentious first moves into the hotel, Vaggie's initial impulse was to get rid of the Egg Boiz, leaving the task to Alastor. Though she insists Alastor remove the little eggies in a humane way, who knows what violent ends they would've met if the Radio Demon had been left to his own devices. Fortunately, Frank lives on, and here's a deviled egg dish to capture his goofy, lovable vibe on a plate.

6 hard-boiled eggs, peeled and halved

½ cup Kewpie mayonnaise

1 teaspoon Dijon mustard

¼ teaspoon smoked paprika

12 black olives, halved

1½ teaspoons edible gold luster dust

12 pinches edible gold flakes

Gently scoop the yolks out of the egg whites. In a small bowl, combine the yolks, mayonnaise, mustard, and paprika. Stir until the mixture is cohesive and smooth.

Brush the outside of the egg whites with gold luster dust; then fill them with the yolk mixture. Add two black olive halves per deviled egg to create eyes. Finish by sprinkling a pinch of gold flakes on top of each egg.

Lucifer's Rubber Duckies

GF, DF ♥ YIELD: 2 SERVINGS

When Lucifer makes his first appearance, we learn a lot about him, including his anxiety about being a good dad, his flair for showmanship—and the fact that his space is covered in rubber ducks. Just . . . so many ducks. It's possible Lucifer needs a more enriching hobby, but in the meantime, here's some duck confit for the King of Hell. Maybe his fire-breathing duckie can help with the roasting.

- 2 duck legs, about ½ pound each
- 1 teaspoon salt
- Freshly ground black pepper

Preheat the oven to 300°F.

Using the tip of a knife or a cocktail skewer, poke small holes all over the skin of the duck legs. Coat the skin with salt and put the legs in a small casserole dish (the snugger the better, to contain the fat). Let sit uncovered at room temperature for 1 hour.

Bake in the oven for 2 hours, or until the skin starts to crisp and brown. Increase the heat to 375°F for 15 minutes, or until the internal temperature of the legs reaches 165°F.

Remove from the oven, season with pepper to taste, and let rest for 15 minutes before plating.

MORNINGSTAR SALAD

V, GF ♥ YIELD: 2 SERVINGS

Charlie sees the good inside every single Sinner. Her goal in rehabilitation is not just changing what Sinners do but how they take care of themselves and others. Join Charlie's effort and try this beet salad—decidedly red, juicy, and packed with vitamins and good vibes! Charlie would be so proud!

2 medium pre-roasted beets, sliced into ¼-inch-thick wheels

DRESSING

1 tablespoon Dijon mustard

½ cup extra-virgin olive oil

1½ fresh lemons, zested and juiced

1 shallot, finely chopped

1 garlic clove, finely chopped

YOGURT SAUCE

4 ounces crumbled feta

1 cup plain Greek yogurt

Salt

Freshly ground black pepper

½ teaspoon chopped mint

SPECIAL EQUIPMENT

Blender

Preheat the oven to 425°F.

Put the beets on a baking sheet and bake in the oven for 2 to 5 minutes, or until warmed through.

TO MAKE THE DRESSING: In a medium mixing bowl, combine the mustard, olive oil, zest and juice of 1 lemon, the shallot, and garlic. Mix well. Once the beets are warm, toss in the dressing and plate.

TO MAKE THE YOGURT SAUCE: In a blender, combine half the feta with the Greek yogurt and juice from the remaining ½ lemon. Add salt and pepper to taste. Dollop the yogurt sauce over the beets. Top with mint and the remaining crumbled feta and serve.

CHARLIE'S CORDIAL CAKE

V ♥ YIELD: ABOUT 10 SERVINGS

Whether welcoming new residents like Sir Pentious or nervously greeting her father for a visit, Charlie does her best to ensure the hotel makes a good first impression. And hey, what's more welcoming than a nice cake? Celebrate Charlotte's complicated family history with this angel food cake dyed red to represent the fire and chaos of her hellish home.

CAKE

1½ cups egg whites

1½ cups sifted powdered sugar

1 cup sifted cake flour

¼ teaspoon salt

1½ teaspoons cream of tartar

About 30 drops red food coloring

1 cup granulated sugar

1 teaspoon pure vanilla extract

2 cups heavy (whipping) cream

RED FROSTING

¼ cup powdered sugar

1 to 4 teaspoons whole milk

3 to 5 drops red food coloring

TO MAKE THE CAKE: In a large bowl, bring the egg whites to room temperature, about 1 hour, outside the refrigerator.

Preheat the oven to 350°F.

In a medium bowl, combine the powdered sugar, cake flour, and salt. Set aside.

In another medium bowl, beat the egg whites until frothy. Add the cream of tartar and food coloring and beat until soft peaks form. Gradually add the granulated sugar, continuing to beat until droopy peaks form and the mixture thickens. Beat in the vanilla.

Sprinkle one-quarter of the dry ingredients over the egg white mixture, gently folding them in with a rubber spatula. Add the remaining dry mixture a little at a time.

Pour the batter into a 10-inch ungreased tube pan and bake in the oven for 40 minutes, or until the top is golden brown and a toothpick inserted comes out clean.

While the cake bakes, in a medium bowl, whip the heavy cream until stiff peaks form.

Once the cake is baked, run a knife around the edge of the pan, and turn out the cake. Let it cool before topping with the whipped cream.

TO MAKE THE RED FROSTING: Sift the sugar into a small bowl and then slowly add 1 teaspoon of milk at a time, until the frosting reaches a silky, loose consistency that is easy to drizzle. Stir in the red food coloring until the desired color is achieved.

Drizzle the "bloody" frosting over the cake.

Angel's Hair Pasta

GF* ♥ YIELD: ABOUT 10 SERVINGS

If anyone at the hotel is going to prefer a liquid diet—I'm talking alcohol people, get your minds out of the gutter!—it's Angel Dust. But even Hell's biggest porn star needs to eat every once in a while, so why not go for a recipe that can appeal to his ego? And you can appeal to that liquid thirst with this robust vodka sauce featuring prosciutto, garlic, and plenty of fresh herbs.

½ cup unsalted butter
½ yellow onion, finely chopped
6 slices (about 2 ounces) prosciutto, coarsely torn
½ cup vodka
One 28-ounce can crushed tomatoes
One 28-ounce can tomato sauce
One 6-ounce can tomato paste
1 tablespoon dried parsley
1 tablespoon dried basil
1 tablespoon dried oregano
1 teaspoon dried fennel
5 garlic cloves
Salt
Freshly ground black pepper
1 teaspoon to 1 tablespoon sugar (optional)
2 cups half-and-half
1 box angel hair pasta
10 basil sprigs, for garnish

In a Dutch oven, heat the butter and chopped onion over medium heat, stirring until the onion is softened and the butter is completely melted. Add the prosciutto and stir until crispy.

Once the prosciutto is crispy, turn the heat to medium-high and add the vodka. Stir until the vodka has evaporated, about 2 to 4 minutes; then reduce the heat to medium.

Add the crushed tomatoes, tomato sauce, and tomato paste. Season with the parsley, basil, oregano, fennel, garlic cloves, and salt and pepper to taste. Stir and then reduce the heat to simmer at the lowest possible setting and cover, simmering for 2 hours. Stir again and taste. To cut any sharp, acidic taste, add 1 teaspoon to 1 tablespoon of sugar, according to preference.

Cover and let simmer until the garlic cloves can be smashed with a wooden spoon. Add the half-and-half and season with salt and pepper to taste.

Serve over angel hair pasta and garnish each plate with a fresh basil sprig.

NOTE: To easily make this recipe gluten free, serve with gluten-free pasta.

Adam's Ribs

GF, DF ♥ YIELD: 1 SERVING

Adam, self-proclaimed Original Dick, has so little regard for his first meeting with Charlie Morningstar, pranking her multiple times throughout, even as he offers her lunch—his personal favorite, a plate of ribs. Get a taste with this recipe for slow-cooked, homemade-barbecue-sauce slathered ribs that we guarantee you'll *love* as much as Adam loves himself.

DRY RUB

½ teaspoon garlic powder

½ teaspoon salt

½ teaspoon onion salt

1 dash freshly ground black pepper

RIBS

Half rack PORK ribs

1¼ cups Mexican lager

BBQ SAUCE

½ cup unsalted butter

1¼ cups ketchup

¾ cup Mexican lager

¾ cup maple syrup

½ cup brown sugar, unpacked

¼ cup apple cider vinegar

¼ cup honey mustard

5 ounces Worcestershire sauce

1½ ounces liquid smoke

TO MAKE THE DRY RUB: In a small bowl, combine the garlic powder, salt, onion salt, and pepper.

TO MAKE THE RIBS: Preheat the oven or grill to 225°F. Rub the ribs with the dry rub. Put the ribs on the rack, bone-side down, and cook for 3 hours. After 3 hours, remove from the oven or grill and wrap in tinfoil with the lager. Wrap securely and put back in oven or on the grill, flesh-side down, for 2 hours.

TO MAKE THE BBQ SAUCE: In the meantime, in a large saucepan, melt the butter. Add the ketchup, Mexican lager, maple syrup, brown sugar, apple cider vinegar, honey mustard, Worcestershire sauce, and liquid smoke and stir. Simmer until thickened. Store excess sauce in a sealed container in the fridge for up to 1 week.

TO FINISH: Remove the ribs from the foil and brush them generously with the homemade BBQ sauce or your favorite store-bought brand. Put back in the oven or on the grill, bone-side down, for 1 more hour, or until the internal temperature of the ribs is 160°F. Add more BBQ sauce to serve.

CANNIBAL TOWN CUISINE

BRAIN FOOD

V, GF ♥ YIELD: 24 SERVINGS

It doesn't matter how pleasant, cordial, or put-together they act; at the end of the day, the residents of Cannibal Town are, well . . . cannibals. But as far as Charlie is concerned, that doesn't mean they can't do their best to better themselves like every other Sinner in Hell! Inspire that mental growth with a bit of brain food, which, you know, the cannibals would probably take issue with the substitutions, but you'll likely enjoy this dessert version a lot more.

- ½ cup milk or dark chocolate chips
- 24 ~~brains~~ PECAN HALVES
- 12 large pitted dates, halved
- ¼ cup smooth peanut butter
- ½ cup ~~blood~~ RED FROSTING (page 126)

In a microwave-safe bowl, microwave the chocolate chips in 30-second increments until almost melted; then stir until they melt throughout. Smear the smooth side of the pecans with the melted chocolate. Set aside.

Fill the inside of the date halves with peanut butter. Add one pecan on top of one peanut butter–filled date, smooth-side down, using the chocolate as an adhesive. Repeat for each date half.

Put the dates on a wax paper–lined baking sheet and freeze for at least 1 hour, up to 24 hours. To serve, drizzle with red frosting drips to resemble blood.

Leftovers can be stored in an airtight container in the freezer.

Cannibal Town–Style Chili

GF ♥ YIELD: ABOUT 12 SERVINGS

Following the battle with the exorcists, there were plenty of dead angels littering the grounds around the ruined hotel. Though Lucifer and KeeKee were able to fix the hotel, one has to imagine the cannibal forces were happy to take care of all those corpses after working up an appetite in battle. Make the most of any meat you've got lying around—in your fridge, of course—with this hearty chili dish, perfect for sating your hunger after a busy day.

1 teaspoon olive oil

½ yellow onion, finely chopped

1 pound lean ground ~~meat~~ BEEF!

One 14.5-ounce can diced tomatoes

One 15.5-ounce can kidney beans

One 15.5-ounce can pinto beans

One 15.5-ounce can black beans

One 15.25-ounce can whole corn kernels

One 15-ounce can tomato sauce

1 teaspoon ground cumin

2 cinnamon sticks, halved

Greek yogurt, for serving

12 cilantro sprigs, chopped, for serving

SPECIAL EQUIPMENT

Blender

In a Dutch oven, combine the olive oil, onion, and ground beef. Stir until the beef is cooked through.

Meanwhile, in a blender, coarsely blend the diced tomatoes and then add to a Dutch oven. Add all the beans, corn, and tomato sauce. Stir. Season with the cumin and cinnamon sticks and stir. Bring to a boil and then reduce to a simmer. Cover and stir periodically for 2 hours.

Serve with a dollop of plain Greek yogurt per bowl and sprinkle each with cilantro.

Crispy Eyeballs

V+, GF, DF ♥ YIELD: 2 SERVINGS

When Charlie raises an army to stand against the forces of Heaven, the majority of her soldiers are from Cannibal Town. Though great allies, their preferred diet leaves a lot to be desired. If you'd ask them, they may suggest that the best finger food—other than, well, actual fingers—would be something easy to pop back by the handful, like crispy eyeballs! This reworked recipe importantly replaces eyeballs with chickpeas. Much easier to source!

- One 15.5-ounce can ~~eyeballs~~ CHICKPEAS
- ½ cup garlic-infused olive oil
- Salt
- Freshly ground black pepper

In a large zip-top plastic bag, combine the chickpeas, olive oil, and salt and pepper to taste. Toss to coat. Let sit in the refrigerator overnight.

Preheat the oven to 450°F.

Spread the seasoned chickpeas in a nonstick casserole dish. Bake for 20 minutes, or until crispy, checking periodically to stir.

Bone Marrow Flute

DF ♥ YIELD: 1 SERVING

While strolling through Cannibal Town, Charlie witnesses the residents of Cannibal Town making the most out of every wayward soul they get their razor-sharp teeth into. Bone marrow can make for a delicious glaze on whatever limb or lung they're snacking on—make the most of your own bite with this recipe for bone marrow shanks, now with 100 percent less human!

2 bone marrow shanks, canoed

⅛ teaspoon salt, plus more as needed

1 small baguette, sliced on the diagonal

1 teaspoon olive oil

1 pinch freshly ground black pepper

1 tablespoon fresh parsley

2 tablespoons fig jam

2 fresh figs, halved

Preheat the oven to 450°F.

Season the bone marrow lightly with salt. Put on a baking sheet and bake for about 10 minutes. Remove the baking sheet from the oven and arrange the baguette slices next to the bone marrow and drizzle with olive oil.

Bake together for 5 minutes more or until the marrow becomes soft but doesn't drip. Season again with salt and pepper and sprinkle with parsley.

To serve, smear the fig jam on one side of a plate, arrange the marrow and bread slices, and scatter the fig halves for garnish.

Pulled Shoulder Nachos

YIELD: 1 SERVING

As leader of Cannibal Town, it's Rosie's job to hear out her residents and make sure they don't get too destructive with their bloody tendencies. Her emporium goes a long way in keeping things orderly, with plenty of cannibal-friendly snacks. Of course, Charlie's no fan of the pinkie fingers Rosie offers her, so here's a more traditional finger food for the non-cannibal crowd to enjoy. Still, plenty of meat in these nachos, and not a bit of it human!

CARNITAS

1 pound PORK shoulder

Salt

Freshly ground black pepper

Olive oil, for drizzling

½ yellow onion, finely chopped

1 cup chicken broth

½ cup orange juice

4 garlic cloves

½ teaspoon garlic olive oil

½ bag ~~severed fingers~~ TORTILLA CHIPS

OPTIONAL TOPPINGS

¼ cup guacamole (page 120)

¼ cup salsa

¼ cup chili con queso

1 dollop plain Greek yogurt

½ teaspoon chopped fresh cilantro

SPECIAL EQUIPMENT

Slow cooker

TO MAKE THE CARNITAS: Season all sides of the pork shoulder with salt and pepper. Drizzle the slow cooker with olive oil, then combine yellow onion, chicken broth, orange juice, and garlic cloves in a slow cooker set on low heat. Cook for 6 hours.

TO MAKE THE NACHOS: Once the carnitas are ready, heat a cast-iron skillet over medium heat. Heat the garlic olive oil in the skillet; then add the carnitas and increase the heat to medium-high. Stir, allowing the meat to crisp. Season with more salt to taste.

Plate the chips and cover with the carnitas. Top with your favorite nacho toppings.

Angel Wings

YIELD: ABOUT 2 SERVINGS

When Charlie recruits the cannibals, they make it clear that they'd love nothing more than to get a taste of the angels they'll be fighting. Well, given that Hazbin Hotel won the battle, you have to imagine those cannibals got their wish. Celebrate the hotel's sweet-and-spicy victory with these hot honey chicken wings!

WINGS

1 tablespoon garlic powder

1 tablespoon onion powder

1 tablespoon salt

1 teaspoon freshly ground black pepper

1½ to 2 pounds ~~angel~~ wings
CHICKEN

HOT HONEY SAUCE

4 tablespoons butter

⅓ cup hot sauce

½ cup honey

1 teaspoon salt

SPECIAL EQUIPMENT

Air fryer

TO MAKE THE WINGS: In a large bowl, stir the garlic powder, onion powder, salt, and pepper until combined. Add the wings, making sure each is coated thoroughly in the mixture. Lay the wings on a drying rack and leave in the refrigerator, uncovered, for 24 hours.

Preheat an air fryer to 400°F.

Put the wings in the air fryer in an even layer, not touching, and cook for 20 minutes, or until fully cooked, with an internal temperature of 165°F.

TO MAKE THE HOT HONEY SAUCE: Meanwhile, in a saucepan, combine the butter, hot sauce, honey, and salt and bring to a slow simmer. Let the sauce thicken before removing it from the heat.

TO FINISH: Put the wings in a medium bowl and coat them in the sauce, reserving a little extra for dipping.

Measurement Conversions

CUPS	TABLESPOONS	TEASPOONS	FLUID OUNCES
1/16 cup	1 tablespoon	3 teaspoons	½ fluid ounce
⅛ cup	2 tablespoons	6 teaspoons	1 fluid ounce
¼ cup	4 tablespoons	12 teaspoons	2 fluid ounces
⅓ cup	5½ tablespoons	16 teaspoons	2⅔ fluid ounces
½ cup	8 tablespoons	24 teaspoons	4 fluid ounces
⅔ cup	10⅔ tablespoons	32 teaspoons	5⅓ fluid ounces
¾ cup	12 tablespoons	36 teaspoons	6 fluid ounces
1 cup	16 tablespoons	48 teaspoons	8 fluid ounces

GALLONS	QUARTS	PINTS	CUPS	FLUID OUNCES
1/16 gallon	¼ quart	½ pint	1 cup	8 fluid ounces
⅛ gallon	½ quart	1 pint	2 cups	16 fluid ounces
¼ gallon	1 quart	2 pints	4 cups	32 fluid ounces
½ gallon	2 quarts	4 pints	8 cups	64 fluid ounces
1 gallon	4 quarts	8 pints	16 cups	128 fluid ounces

GRAMS	OUNCES
14 grams	½ ounce
28 grams	1 ounce
57 grams	2 ounces
85 grams	3 ounces
113 grams	4 ounces
142 grams	5 ounces
170 grams	6 ounces
283 grams	10 ounces
397 grams	14 ounces
454 grams	16 ounces
907 grams	32 ounces

IMPERIAL	METRIC
1 inch	2.5 centimeters
2 inches	5 centimeters
4 inches	10 centimeters
6 inches	15 centimeters
8 inches	20 centimeters
10 inches	25 centimeters

FAHRENHEIT	CELSIUS
200°F	93°C
225°F	107°C
250°F	121°C
275°F	135°C
300°F	149°C
325°F	163°C
350°F	177°C
375°F	191°C
400°F	204°C
425°F	218°C
450°F	232°C

About the Authors

Thea Engst is a cocktail developer and author of *Sex and the City Cocktails* and *Spirits of the Tarot* (for which she won a Readable Feast Award) and coauthor of *Nectar of the Gods* and *Drink Like a Bartender*. She developed recipes for a bubbly cocktail card deck as well as for the *Unofficial Disney Parks* cookbooks. Thea worked in hospitality for more than a decade and is a published poet with an MFA from Emerson College. She currently resides in Cambridge, MA with her cat Nox. Find her on Instagram and TikTok @theaengstauthor.

Jordan Alsaqa (he/him) is a Palestinian-American comic and pop culture writer. Jordan's work spans numerous genres across a variety of publishers, including *Raise Hell!*, *Cooking with Monsters*, and *Bullet Adventures*. He has previously written cookbooks for franchises such as Apex Legends and Borderlands. Currently, Jordan is working on *Affairs of the Haunt*, a haunted romance co-created with artist Kaylee Rowena from Andrews McMeel.

Acknowledgments

This book would not have been possible without the love and support of my dear friend, Michaela, who cheers me on every second of every day—especially during the development of these recipes. Michaela, you are the friend who everyone needs in their life to achieve their dreams, thank you. I'd also like to thank my siblings and their spouses: Lea, Lisbeth, John, Lauren, Maty, Stefan, and Rena; my aunties Nancy and Hayne; and my parents. Thank you all for loving this hazbin exactly as I am.

Thea Engst

Thanks to Maeve, my agent, for always having my back and helping me find cool projects like this one. Thanks to Sami, for inviting me to work on this project, and to Jennifer, for being my first editorial connection at Insight Editions. And, as always, a huge thanks to my fiancé Liz for always supporting my writing career.

Jordan Alsaqa

INDEX

INSIGHT
EDITIONS

PO Box 3088
San Rafael, CA 94912
www.insighteditions.com

Find us on Facebook: www.facebook.com/InsightEditions
Follow us on Instagram: @insighteditions

ISBN: 979-8-3374-0263-5

Publisher: Raoul Goff
SVP, Group Publisher: Vanessa Lopez
VP, Manufacturing: Alix Nicholaeff
Editorial Director: Thom O'Hearn
Art Director: Stuart Smith
Senior Designer: Brooke McCullum
Associate Editor: Sami Alvarado
Managing Editor: Shannon Ballesteros
Managing Editorial Assistant: Lindsay Gibson
Editorial Assistant: Melissa Santoyo
Production Manager: Deena Hashem
Strategic Production Planner: Lina s Palma-Temena

Photography by Carla Choy

ROOTS of PEACE
REPLANTED PAPER

Insight Editions, in association with Roots of Peace, will plant two trees for each tree used in the manufacturing of this book. Roots of Peace is an internationally renowned humanitarian organization dedicated to eradicating land mines worldwide and converting war-torn lands into productive farms and wildlife habitats. Roots of Peace will plant two million fruit and nut trees in Afghanistan and provide farmers there with the skills and support necessary for sustainable land use.

Manufactured in China by Insight Editions

10 9 8 7 6 5 4 3 2 1